VEGETARIAN CLASSICS

Consultant Editor:
Valerie Ferguson

Contents

Introduction

Vegetarian food has never been so exciting. Supermarkets are filled with fresh produce from all over the world, so it is amazingly easy to create imaginative, nourishing and, above all, delicious vegetarian meals for all occasions and at any time of year. Individual vegetables may take the starring role in a dish or they may be mixed together and served with pasta or rice to make a glorious and colourful combination. Pulses, cheese and other dairy products, eggs, nuts, seeds and tofu are all essentials in the vegetarian store cupboard, providing almost infinite variety in the daily diet.

The secret of a well-balanced vegetarian diet is the same as any other diet – a wide variety of different types of food to ensure an adequate daily intake of all essential nutrients. Wherever possible, include fresh fruit, fruit juice and fresh vegetables, especially leafy greens, with each meal.

Each day, aim to eat a good selection of grains, such as oats, wheat and barley, pasta, rice and high-fibre breakfast cereals, breads and potatoes, pulses and legumes, such as lentils, canned or dried beans and peas. Aim for a moderate daily intake of dried fruits and unsalted nuts, cheese, especially high-fat types, and oils (use unsaturated ones such as olive, sunflower, corn or peanut as much as possible), margarine, butter and cream.

The Vegetarian Larder

The store cupboard ingredients listed below provide the basis for a huge range of tasty and nutritious vegetarian dishes.

FLOURS

Flour is a good source of protein and complex carbohydrates. Use different types, mixing wholemeal and plain flours to make pastry and bread.

RICE & GRAINS

Brown and wholegrain rices provide more dietary fibre than white rice. Basmati and long grain rices are good in all sorts of dishes. Wild rice, which is not a real rice but a type of grass, has good levels of proteins.

Useful as an alternative to rice, grains include barley, wheat berries, couscous, millet, quinoa and buckwheat. Grains are a useful source of protein and carbohydrate.

PULSES

Although high in protein, pulses lack one of the essential amino acids. However, grain foods, despite missing two different amino acids, do have this essential one so, eaten together, grains and pulses make a complete protein. When you eat pulses, therefore, try to include grain foods in the same meal – for example, lentils with rice, beans with pasta or hummus with bread.

Pulses generally need presoaking. Remember to boil them fast for the first 10 minutes of cooking to destroy any mild toxins present, then lower the heat and simmer gently.

Some lentils, can be cooked without presoaking – split red lentils take just 20 minutes to cook and are excellent as a thickener for soups and stews.

Beans are perfect for soups, pâtés and purées. There are lots of varieties: try butter beans, kidney beans, cannellini beans or pinto beans.

PASTA

A good source of complex carbohydrates, pasta is quick and easy to cook, and there is a multitude of shapes and colours to add variety. Wholewheat pastas have a slightly nutty taste and chewy texture.

OILS, VINEGARS & FLAVOURINGS

For general use choose oils high in polyunsaturates: sunflower, rapeseed and groundnut oils have a very light flavour, while corn, walnut, hazelnut and sesame oils have a stronger taste. Olive oil, prized for its flavour, is also high in monosaturates which are thought to help reduce blood cholesterol levels. Fats and oils contribute vital vitamins such as A, D and E, so even if you are counting calories don't cut them out altogether.

White, or red wine and sherry vinegars are ideal for salads. Balsamic has a distinctive sweet/sour flavour which can be used in salad dressings

or to liven up roasted vegetables and cooked grains. Different types of mustards, such as Dijon or wholegrain, can also add zest to your cooking.

NUTS & SEEDS
These high-protein foods are delicious in all sorts of recipes. The most popular nuts are peanuts, walnuts, almonds, cashews and pistachios. For maximum flavour, lightly roast nuts before chopping. There's an increasing range of seeds readily available – most useful are sunflower and sesame seeds, though poppy seeds and caraway seeds are also delicious.

HERBS & SPICES
Fresh or dried herbs and aromatic spices lift even the most ordinary vegetarian dishes. Replace dried herbs regularly and store away from the light. Fresh herbs are best stored in polythene bags in the fridge. Toast spices in a dry frying pan, before adding to a recipe, to bring out the full flavours.

BOTTLED & CANNED GOODS
Indispensable items for your store cupboard include canned pulses and vegetables, pesto, soy sauce, vegetable granules or stock cubes, sun-dried tomatoes, tomato purée and tahini.

Techniques

PREPARING GARLIC

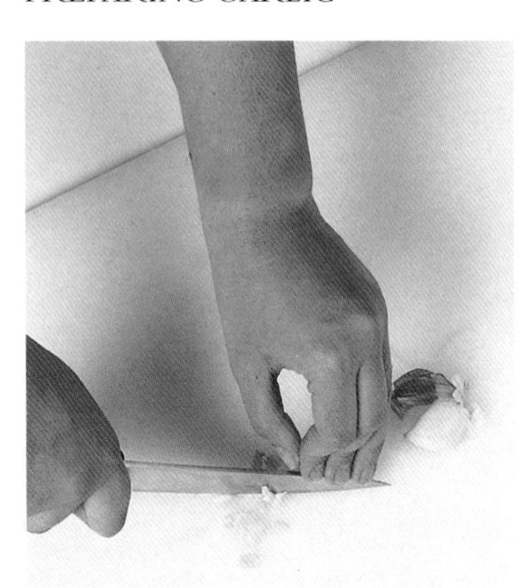

1 Break off the clove of garlic, place the flat side of a large knife on top and strike with your fist. Remove all the papery outer skin. Begin by finely chopping the clove.

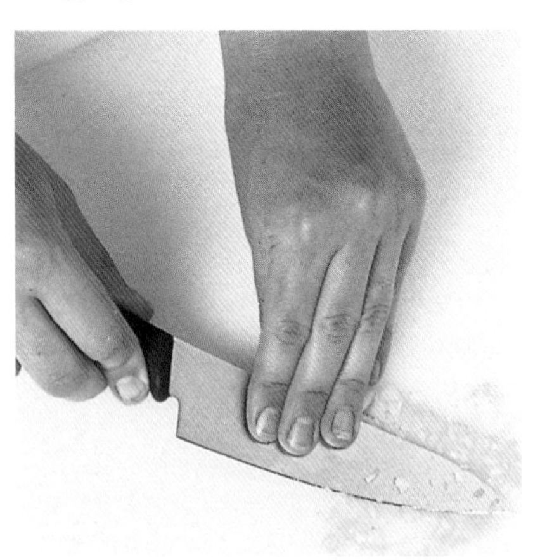

2 Sprinkle over a little table salt and, using the flat side of a large knife blade, work the salt into the garlic, until the clove softens and releases its juices. Use as required.

CHOPPING HERBS

1 To chop fresh herbs: hold the leaves or sprigs together in a bunch and chop coarsely using a sharp knife. Continue chopping the herbs until they are fine.

2 Alternatively, use a herb chopper (also called a mezzaluna) and chop in the same way as above.

GRINDING SPICES

Some spices are used whole, but where they are crushed or ground, the best flavour will be obtained if you start off with whole spices and crush them as and when needed.

1 If preparing a large quantity of spices, use a coffee grinder.

2 Alternatively, use a pestle and mortar, especially if grinding small quantities.

MAKING VEGETABLE STOCK

A useful basic stock for soups, risottos and sauces.

Makes about 1.5 litres/2½ pints/ 6¼ cups

INGREDIENTS
1 onion
2 carrots
2 large celery sticks, plus small amounts of any of the following: leek, celeriac, parsnip, turnip, cabbage or cauliflower trimmings, mushroom peelings
1 bouquet garni
6 black peppercorns
30 ml/2 tbsp vegetable oil

1 Peel, halve and slice the onion. Peel and roughly chop the remaining vegetables.

2 Heat the oil in a large pan and fry the onion and vegetables until soft and lightly browned. Add the remaining ingredients and cover with 1.75 litres/3 pints/7½ cups water.

3 Bring to the boil, skim the surface, then partially cover and simmer for 1½ hours. Strain the stock and allow to cool. Store in the fridge for 2–3 days.

Minestrone with Pesto

Minestrone is a thick, mixed vegetable soup using almost any combination of seasonal vegetables. Short pasta or rice may also be added.

Serves 6

INGREDIENTS
1.5 litres/2½ pints/6¼ cups vegetable stock or water or a combination of both
45ml/3 tbsp olive oil
1 large onion, finely chopped
1 leek, sliced
2 carrots, finely chopped
1 celery stick, finely chopped
2 garlic cloves, finely chopped
2 potatoes, peeled and cut into small dice
1 bay leaf
1 fresh thyme sprig or 1.5 ml/¼ tsp dried thyme
115 g/4 oz/1 cup peas, fresh or frozen
2–3 courgettes, finely chopped
3 medium tomatoes, peeled and finely chopped
425 g/15 oz/2 cups cooked or canned beans such as cannellini
45 ml/3 tbsp pesto sauce
salt and freshly ground black pepper
grated Parmesan cheese, to serve

1 In a medium saucepan, heat the stock or water to simmering.

2 In another saucepan, heat the olive oil. Stir in the onion and leek and cook for 5–6 minutes, or until the onion softens. Add the carrots, celery and garlic and cook over moderate heat, stirring frequently, for another 5 minutes.

3 Add the potatoes and cook for 2–3 minutes, then pour in the hot stock or water and stir well. Add the herbs and season with salt and pepper. Bring to the boil, reduce the heat slightly and cook for 10–12 minutes.

4 Stir in the peas, if using fresh ones, and the courgettes. Simmer for 5 minutes more. If using frozen peas, add them now along with the tomatoes. Cover the pan and simmer for 5–8 minutes or until the vegetables are tender.

5 About 10 minutes before serving the soup, remove the lid and stir in the beans. Simmer for 10 minutes. Stir in the pesto sauce. Taste for seasoning. Simmer for another 5 minutes, then remove from the heat. Allow the soup to stand for a few minutes before serving with the grated Parmesan.

Pea, Leek & Broccoli Soup

A delicious and nutritious soup, ideal for warming you on those dark and chilly winter evenings.

Serves 4–6

INGREDIENTS
1 onion, chopped
225 g/8 oz/2 cups leeks (trimmed weight), sliced
225 g/8 oz/1⅓ cups unpeeled potatoes, diced
900 ml/1½ pints/3¾ cups vegetable stock
1 bay leaf
225 g/8 oz/1½ cups broccoli florets
175 g/6 oz/1½ cups frozen peas
30–45 ml/2–3 tbsp chopped fresh parsley
salt and freshly ground black pepper
parsley leaves, to garnish

1 Put the onion, leeks, potatoes, stock and bay leaf in a large saucepan and mix together. Cover, bring to the boil and simmer for 10 minutes, stirring.

2 Add the broccoli and peas. Cover, return to the boil and simmer for a further 10 minutes, stirring occasionally.

3 Set aside to cool slightly and remove and discard the bay leaf. Purée the soup in a blender or food processor until smooth.

4 Add the chopped parsley, season to taste and process briefly. Return to the saucepan and reheat gently until piping hot. Ladle into soup bowls, garnish with parsley leaves and serve.

COOK'S TIP: You could cut the vegetables finely and leave the soup chunky rather than puréeing it.

Carrot & Coriander Soup

If possible, use a good home-made stock for this soup – it adds a far greater depth of flavour than stock made from cubes.

Serves 4

INGREDIENTS
50 g/2 oz/¼ cup butter
3 leeks, sliced
450 g/1 lb/ 4 cups carrots, sliced
15 ml/1 tbsp ground coriander
1.2 litres/2 pints/5 cups vegetable stock
150 ml/¼ pint/⅔ cup Greek-style yogurt
salt and freshly ground black pepper
30–45 ml/2–3 tbsp chopped fresh coriander, to garnish

1 Melt the butter in a large pan. Add the leeks and carrots and stir well, coating the vegetables with the butter. Cover and cook for about 10 minutes, until the vegetables are beginning to soften but not colour.

2 Stir in the ground coriander and cook for about 1 minute. Pour in the stock and add seasoning to taste. Bring to the boil, cover and simmer for about 20 minutes, until the leeks and carrots are tender.

3 Leave to cool slightly, then purée the soup in a blender until smooth. Return the soup to the pan and add 30 ml/2 tbsp of the yogurt, then taste the soup and adjust the seasoning. Reheat gently but do not boil.

4 Ladle the soup into four bowls and put a spoonful of the remaining yogurt in the centre of each. Scatter over the chopped fresh coriander and serve immediately.

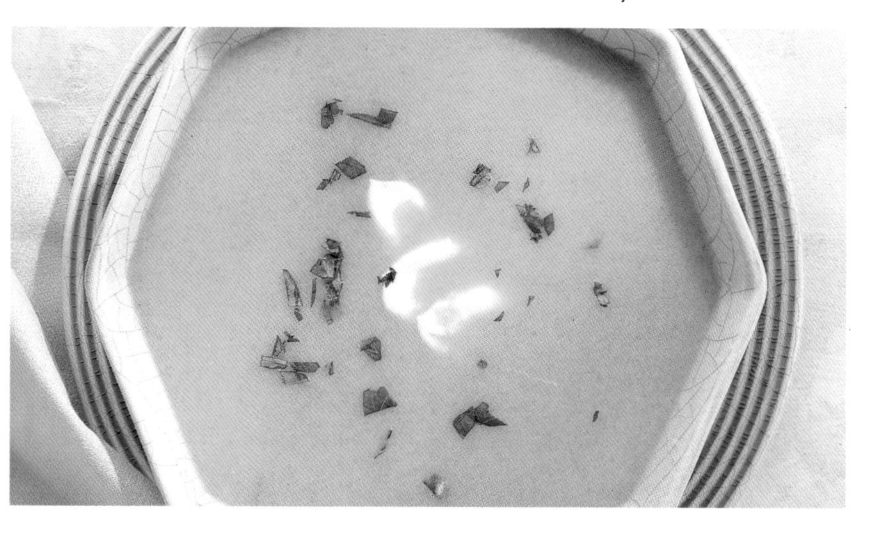

Stuffed Vine Leaves

Based on the Greek dolmas (or dolmades) but with a wholegrain vegetarian stuffing, this makes an excellent starter, snack or buffet dish.

Makes about 40

INGREDIENTS
15 ml/1 tbsp sunflower oil
5 ml/1 tsp sesame oil
1 onion, finely chopped
225 g/8 oz/1⅓ cups brown rice
600 ml/1 pint/2½ cups vegetable stock
1 small yellow pepper, seeded and finely chopped
115 g/4 oz/½ cup ready-to-eat dried apricots, finely chopped
2 lemons
50 g/2 oz/½ cup pine nuts
45ml/3 tbsp chopped fresh parsley
30 ml/2 tbsp chopped fresh mint
2.5 ml/½ tsp ground mixed spice
225 g/8 oz packet vine leaves preserved in brine, drained
30 ml/2 tbsp olive oil
salt and freshly ground black pepper
lemon wedges, to garnish

TO SERVE
300 ml/½ pint/1¼ cups natural yogurt
30 ml/2 tbsp chopped fresh mixed herbs
cayenne pepper

1 Heat the sunflower and sesame oils together in a fairly large saucepan. Add the onion and cook gently for 5 minutes to soften.

2 Add the rice, stirring to coat the grains in oil. Pour in the stock, bring to the boil, then lower the heat, cover the pan and simmer for 30 minutes, or until the rice is tender but retains a little "bite".

3 Stir in the chopped yellow pepper and apricots, with a little more stock if necessary. Replace the lid and cook for a further 5 minutes.

4 Grate 1 lemon, then squeeze both lemons. Drain off any stock which has not been absorbed by the rice. Stir in the pine nuts, herbs, mixed spice, lemon rind and half the juice. Season with salt and pepper and set aside.

5 Bring a saucepan of water to the boil and blanch the vine leaves for 5 minutes. Drain the leaves well, then place them shiny side down on a board. Cut out any coarse stalks.

6 Place a small heap of the rice mixture in the centre of each vine leaf. Fold the stem end over, then the sides and roll towards the pointed end to make neat tight parcels. Pack the parcels closely together in a shallow serving dish. Mix the remaining lemon juice with the olive oil. Pour the mixture over the vine leaves, cover and chill.

7 Spoon the yogurt into a bowl, stir in the herbs and sprinkle with cayenne pepper. Garnish the stuffed vine leaves with lemon wedges and serve with the yogurt and herb dip.

COOK'S TIP: You could use the leaves of Swiss chard, young spinach or cabbage instead of vine leaves.

Goat's Cheese Salad with Buckwheat, Fresh Figs & Walnuts

The robust flavours of goat's cheese and buckwheat combine especially well with ripe figs and walnuts. The olive and walnut oil dressing contains no vinegar and depends instead on the acidity of the cheese.

Serves 4

INGREDIENTS

175 g/6 oz/1 cup couscous
30 ml/2 tbsp toasted buckwheat
1 egg, hard-boiled
30 ml/2 tbsp chopped fresh parsley
60 ml/4 tbsp olive oil
45ml/3 tbsp walnut oil
115 g/4 oz rocket
½ frisée lettuce
175 g/6 oz/1½ cups crumbly white goat's cheese
50 g/2 oz/½ cup broken walnuts, toasted
4 ripe figs, trimmed and almost cut into four (leave the pieces joined at the base)

1 Place the couscous and buckwheat in a bowl, cover with boiling water and leave to soak for 15 minutes. Place in a sieve if necessary to drain off any remaining water, then spread out on a metal tray and allow to cool.

2 Shell the hard-boiled egg and pass it through a fine grater. Toss the egg, parsley and couscous mixture in a bowl. Combine the two oils and use half to moisten the mixture.

3 Dress the salad leaves with the remaining oil and distribute them among four large plates.

4 Pile the couscous in the centre, crumble on the goat's cheese, scatter with toasted walnuts and top with the figs.

COOK'S TIP: Choose a strongly flavoured mature goat's cheese with a firm, crumbly texture for this salad.

Tempura Vegetables with Dipping Sauce

A Japanese favourite, these are thinly sliced, fresh vegetables fried in a light, crispy batter and served with a small bowl of flavoured soy sauce.

Serves 4–6

INGREDIENTS
1 medium courgette, cut into thin sticks
1 red pepper, seeded and cut into wedges
3 large mushrooms, quartered
1 fennel bulb, cut into wedges with root attached
½ medium aubergine, thinly sliced
oil, for deep frying

FOR THE DIPPING SAUCE
45 ml/3 tbsp soy sauce
15 ml/1 tbsp medium-dry sherry
5 ml/1 tsp sesame seed oil
a few shreds of fresh root ginger or spring onion

FOR THE BATTER
1 egg
115 g/4 oz/1 cup plain flour
175 ml/6 fl oz/¾ cup cold water
salt and freshly ground black pepper

1 Prepare all the vegetables and lay them out on a tray, together with sheets of kitchen paper for draining them after cooking.

2 Mix the sauce ingredients together by whisking them in a jug or shaking them together in a screw-top jar. Pour into a bowl.

3 Half-fill a deep frying pan with oil and preheat to a temperature of about 190°C/375°F. Quickly whisk the batter ingredients together, but don't overbeat them. It doesn't matter if the batter is a little lumpy.

4 Fry the vegetables in batches by dipping a few quickly into the batter and lowering them into the hot oil in a wire basket. Fry for just 1 minute until golden brown and crisp. Remove from the oil and drain on the kitchen paper. Keep those you have cooked, uncovered, in a warm oven while you fry the rest. Serve the vegetables on a large platter alongside the dipping sauce.

COOK'S TIP: Successful deep frying can be quite tricky and a bit hazardous. Never leave the pan of oil unattended while the heat is turned on.

Penne with Aubergine & Mint Pesto

This splendid variation on the classic Italian pesto uses fresh mint rather than basil for a different flavour.

Serves 4

INGREDIENTS
2 large aubergines
salt
450 g/1 lb penne
50 g/2 oz/½ cup walnut halves

FOR THE MINT PESTO
25 g/1 oz/½ cup fresh mint
15 g/½ oz/¼ cup fresh flat-leaf parsley
40 g/1½ oz/⅓ cup walnuts
40 g/1½ oz/½ cup Parmesan cheese, finely grated
2 garlic cloves
90 ml/6 tbsp olive oil
salt and freshly ground black pepper

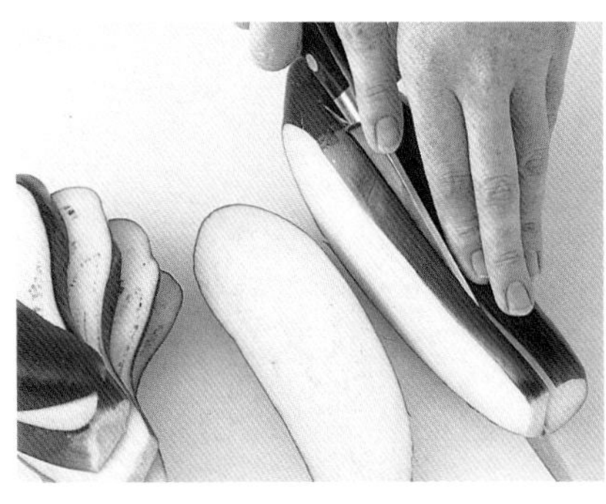

1 Cut the aubergines lengthways into 1 cm/½ in slices.

2 Cut the slices again crossways to give short strips.

3 Layer the aubergine strips in a colander with salt and leave to stand for 30 minutes over a plate to catch any juices. Rinse well in cold water and drain.

4 Place all the pesto ingredients, except the oil, in a blender or food processor, blend until smooth, then gradually add the oil in a thin stream until the mixture amalgamates. Season to taste.

5 Cook the penne, following the instructions on the packet, for about 8 minutes, or until nearly cooked. Add the aubergine and cook for a further 3 minutes.

6 Drain well and toss in the mint pesto and walnut halves and mix well. Serve immediately.

Baked Vegetable Lasagne

This is a vegetarian version of the classic pasta dish.

Serves 8

INGREDIENTS
30 ml/2 tbsp olive oil
1 medium onion, very finely chopped
500 g/1¼ lb tomatoes, fresh or canned, chopped
675 g/1½ lb cultivated or wild mushrooms or a combination of both
175 g/6 oz/¾ cup butter
2 garlic cloves, finely chopped
juice of ½ lemon
75 g/3 oz/¾ cup plain flour
1.2 litres/2 pints/5 cups milk
pinch of grated nutmeg
400 g/14 oz egg lasagne
175 g/6 oz/2 cups Parmesan or Cheddar cheese or a combination of both, grated
salt and freshly ground black pepper
fresh parsley, finely chopped, to garnish

1 Butter a large, shallow baking dish, preferably rectangular or square.

2 In a small frying pan, heat the oil and sauté the onion until translucent. Add the chopped tomatoes and cook for 6–8 minutes, stirring often. Season with salt and pepper and set aside.

3 Wipe the mushrooms carefully with a damp cloth. Slice them finely, and cook in 40 g/1½ oz/3 tbsp of the butter in a frying pan until they start to release their liquid.

4 Add the garlic and lemon juice and season. Cook until the liquid has reduced and the mushrooms are starting to brown. Set aside.

5 Make a béchamel sauce: put 75 g/3 oz/6 tbsp of the butter, the flour and milk into a saucepan and bring slowly to the boil, whisking constantly. The mixture should thicken and become smooth. Season with salt, pepper and nutmeg. Set aside and keep warm.

6 Preheat the oven to 200°C/400°F/Gas 6. Cook the pasta in boiling water as instructed on the packet.

7 To assemble the lasagne, have all the elements at hand. Spread one large spoonful of the béchamel sauce over the bottom of the dish. Arrange a layer of pasta in the dish, cutting it with a sharp knife so that it fits well. Cover the pasta with a thin layer of mushrooms, then one of béchamel sauce. Sprinkle with a little cheese.

8 Make another layer of pasta, spread with a thin layer of tomatoes, and then one of béchamel. Sprinkle with cheese. Repeat the layers, ending with pasta coated with béchamel. Do not make more than six layers of pasta. Sprinkle with cheese and dot with butter. Bake for 20 minutes. Leave to stand for 5 minutes before serving.

Red Onion & Courgette Pizza

It's easy to make a home-made pizza using fast-action dried yeast. You can either add the traditional cheese and tomato topping or try something different, such as the combination described here.

Serves 4

INGREDIENTS
350 g/12 oz/3 cups plain flour
1 sachet easy-blend dried yeast
10 ml/2 tsp salt
lukewarm water, to mix

FOR THE TOPPING
2 red onions, thinly sliced
60 ml/4 tbsp olive oil
2 courgettes, thinly sliced
freshly grated nutmeg
about 115 g/4 oz/½ cup semi-soft goat's cheese
6 sun-dried tomatoes in oil, snipped
dried oregano
salt and freshly ground black pepper

1 Preheat the oven to 200°C/400°F/Gas 6. Mix the flour, yeast and salt together, then mix to a firm dough with warm water. The quantity of water depends on the flour, but start with 150 ml/¼ pint/⅔ cup.

2 Knead the dough for about 5 minutes, until it is smooth and elastic, then roll it out to a large circle and place on a lightly greased baking sheet. Set aside somewhere warm to rise slightly while you make the topping.

3 Gently fry the onions in half the oil for 5 minutes, then add the courgettes and fry for a further 2 minutes. Season and add freshly grated nutmeg to taste.

4 Spread the pizza base with the fried vegetable mixture and dot with the cheese, tomatoes and oregano. Sprinkle over the rest of the oil and bake for 12–15 minutes, until golden and crisp. Serve hot.

Polenta with Mushrooms

This dish is delicious made with a mixture of wild and cultivated mushrooms. Just a few dried porcini mushrooms will help to give a more intense and rich Italian flavour.

Serves 6

INGREDIENTS
10 g/¼ oz/2 tbsp dried porcini mushrooms (omit if using wild mushrooms)
60 ml/4 tbsp olive oil
1 small onion, finely chopped
675 g/1½ lb wild or cultivated mushrooms or a combination of both
2 garlic cloves, finely chopped
45 ml/3 tbsp chopped fresh parsley
3 medium tomatoes, peeled and diced
15 ml/1 tbsp tomato purée
175 ml/6 fl oz/¾ cup warm water
1.5 ml/¼ tsp fresh thyme leaves or a pinch of dried thyme
1 bay leaf
salt and freshly ground black pepper
a few fresh parsley sprigs, to garnish

FOR THE POLENTA
1.5 litres/2½ pints/6¼ cups water
15 ml/1 tbsp salt
350 g/12 oz/2½ cups polenta flour

1 Soak the dried mushrooms, if using, in a small cup of warm water for 20 minutes. Remove the mushrooms with a slotted spoon and rinse them well in several changes of cold water. Filter the soaking water through a layer of kitchen paper placed in a sieve and reserve.

2 In a large frying pan, heat the oil and sauté the onion over low heat until soft and golden.

3 Clean the fresh mushrooms by wiping them with a damp cloth. Cut into slices. When the onion is soft, add the mushrooms to the pan. Stir over moderate to high heat until they release their liquid. Add the garlic, parsley and diced tomatoes. Cook for 4–5 minutes more.

4 Soften the tomato purée in the warm water (use only 120 ml/ 4 fl oz/½ cup water if you are using dried mushrooms). Add it to the pan with the herbs. Add the dried mushrooms and soaking liquid, if using them. Mix well and season with salt and pepper. Lower the heat to low to moderate and cook for 15–20 minutes. Set aside while you make the polenta.

5 Bring the water to the boil in a large, heavy saucepan. Add the salt, reduce the heat to a simmer and add the polenta flour in a fine rain, whisking constantly. Switch to a long-handled wooden spoon and stir the polenta continuously over low heat until it pulls away from the sides of the pan. This may take from 25 to 50 minutes.

6 When the polenta has almost finished cooking, gently reheat the mushroom sauce. To serve, spoon the polenta on to a warmed serving platter. Make a well in the centre. Spoon some of the mushroom sauce into the well and garnish with the fresh parsley sprigs. Serve at once, passing round the remaining mushroom sauce in a separate bowl.

Stir-fried Tofu & Beansprouts with Noodles

Oriental flavours mingle in this easy-to-prepare dish, which makes a tasty and substantial meal.

Serves 4

INGREDIENTS
225 g/8 oz firm tofu
groundnut oil, for deep frying
175 g/6 oz medium egg noodles
15 ml/1 tbsp sesame oil
5 ml/1 tsp cornflour
10 ml/2 tsp dark soy sauce
30 ml/2 tbsp Chinese rice wine
5 ml/1 tsp sugar
6–8 spring onions, cut diagonally into 2.5 cm/1 in lengths
3 garlic cloves, sliced
1 green chilli, seeded and sliced
115 g/4 oz/1 cup Chinese cabbage leaves, coarsely shredded
50 g/2 oz/¼ cup beansprouts
50 g/2 oz/⅓ cup cashew nuts, toasted

1 Drain the tofu and pat dry with kitchen paper. Cut the tofu into 2.5 cm/1 in cubes. Half-fill a large heated wok with groundnut oil and heat to 180°C/350°F. Deep fry the tofu cubes in batches for 1–2 minutes, until golden and crisp. Drain on crumpled kitchen paper. Carefully pour all but 30 ml/2 tbsp of the oil from the wok.

2 Cook the noodles. Rinse them under cold water and drain well. Toss in 10 ml/2 tsp of sesame oil and set aside. In a bowl, blend together the cornflour, soy sauce, rice wine, sugar and remaining sesame oil.

3 Reheat the 30 ml/2 tbsp of groundnut oil and, when hot, add the spring onions, garlic, chilli, Chinese cabbage and beansprouts. Stir-fry for 1–2 minutes.

4 Add the tofu with the noodles and sauce. Cook, stirring, for about 1 minute until well mixed. Sprinkle with the cashew nuts. Serve at once.

Baked Stuffed Aubergines

The name of this famous meze dish, Imam Bayaldi, means "the Imam fainted" – perhaps with pleasure at the deliciousness of the dish. It is eaten all over the Middle East.

Serves 6

INGREDIENTS
3 aubergines
60 ml/4 tbsp olive oil
1 large onion, chopped
1 small red pepper, seeded and diced
1 small green pepper, seeded and diced
3 garlic cloves, crushed
5–6 tomatoes, peeled and chopped
30 ml/2 tbsp chopped fresh parsley
about 250 ml/8 fl oz/1 cup
boiling water
15 ml/1 tbsp lemon juice
salt and freshly ground black pepper
fresh parsley leaves, to garnish
bread, salad and yogurt dip, to serve

1 Preheat the oven to 190°C/375°F/ Gas 5. Cut the aubergines in half lengthways and scoop out the flesh, reserving the shells.

2 Heat 30 ml/2 tbsp of the oil and fry the onion and peppers for 5–6 minutes, until both are slightly softened but not too tender.

3 Add the crushed garlic and continue to cook for a further 2 minutes, then stir in the tomatoes, chopped parsley and aubergine flesh. Season, stir well and fry over a moderate heat for 2–3 minutes.

4 Heat the remaining oil in a separate pan and fry the aubergine shells, two at a time, on both sides.

5 Stuff the shells with the sautéed vegetables. Arrange the aubergines closely together in an ovenproof dish and pour enough boiling water around the aubergines to come half-way up their sides. Cover with foil and bake in the oven for 45–60 minutes, until the aubergines are tender and most of the liquid has been absorbed.

6 Place a half aubergine on each serving plate and sprinkle with lemon juice. Serve hot or cold, garnished with parsley and accompanied by bread, salad and yogurt dip.

COOK'S TIP: This flavourful dish can be made in advance and is ideal for a buffet table. Use smaller aubergines to make serving easier.

Spiced Vegetable Couscous

Couscous, a cereal processed from semolina, is used throughout North Africa, especially in Morocco.

Serves 6

INGREDIENTS
45 ml/3 tbsp vegetable oil
1 large onion, finely chopped
2 garlic cloves, crushed
15 ml/1 tbsp tomato purée
2.5 ml/½ tsp ground turmeric
2.5 ml/½ tsp cayenne pepper
2.5 ml/½ tsp ground coriander
5 ml/1 tsp ground cumin
225 g/8 oz/1½ cups cauliflower florets
225 g/8 oz/1 cup baby carrots, trimmed
1 red pepper, seeded and diced
4 beefsteak tomatoes
225 g/8 oz/1¾ cups courgettes, thickly sliced
400 g/14 oz can chickpeas, drained and rinsed
45 ml/3 tbsp chopped fresh coriander
salt and freshly ground black pepper
fresh coriander sprigs, to garnish

FOR THE COUSCOUS
450 g/1 lb/2⅔ cups couscous
5 ml/1 tsp salt
50 g/2 oz/4 tbsp butter

1 Heat 30 ml/2 tbsp of the oil in a large pan, add the onion and garlic and cook until soft. Stir in the tomato purée, turmeric, cayenne, ground coriander and cumin. Cook, stirring, for 2-3 minutes.

2 Add the cauliflower, carrots and red pepper, with enough water to come half-way up the vegetables. Bring to the boil, then lower the heat, cover and simmer for 10 minutes.

3 Plunge the tomatoes into boiling water for 30 seconds, then refresh in cold water. Peel away the skins and chop the flesh. Add the sliced courgettes, chickpeas and tomatoes to the other vegetables and cook for a further 10 minutes. Stir in the chopped fresh coriander and season with salt and pepper. Keep hot.

4 To cook the couscous, bring 475 ml/16 fl oz/2 cups water to the boil in a large saucepan. Add the remaining oil and the salt. Remove from the heat and add the couscous, stirring. Allow to swell for 2 minutes. Add the butter and heat through gently, stirring to separate the grains.

5 Turn the couscous out on to a warm serving dish and spoon the vegetables on top, pouring over any liquid. Garnish with fresh coriander sprigs and serve immediately.

COOK'S TIP: If you cannot find beefsteak tomatoes you can substitute 6 ordinary tomatoes or a 400 g/14 oz can chopped tomatoes.

Vegetable Fajita

A colourful medley of mushrooms and peppers in a spicy sauce, wrapped in tortillas and served with creamy guacamole.

Serves 2

INGREDIENTS
1 onion
1 red pepper
1 green pepper
1 yellow pepper
1 garlic clove, crushed
225 g/8 oz mushrooms
90 ml/6 tbsp vegetable oil
30 ml/2 tbsp medium chilli powder
salt and freshly ground black pepper
fresh coriander sprigs and 1 lime
cut into wedges, to garnish
4–6 flour tortillas, warmed, to serve

FOR THE GUACAMOLE
1 ripe avocado
1 shallot, roughly chopped
1 green chilli, seeded and roughly chopped
juice of 1 lime

1 Slice the onion. Cut the peppers in half, remove the seeds and cut the flesh into strips. Combine the onion and peppers in a bowl. Add the crushed garlic and mix lightly.

2 Remove the mushroom stalks: save for making stock, or discard. Slice the mushroom caps and add to the pepper mixture in the bowl. Mix the oil and chilli powder in a cup, pour over the vegetable mixture and stir well. Set aside.

3 Make the guacamole. Cut the avocado in half and remove the stone and the peel. Put the flesh into a food processor or blender with the shallot, green chilli and lime juice. Process for 1 minute, until smooth. Scrape into a small bowl, cover closely and put in the fridge to chill until required.

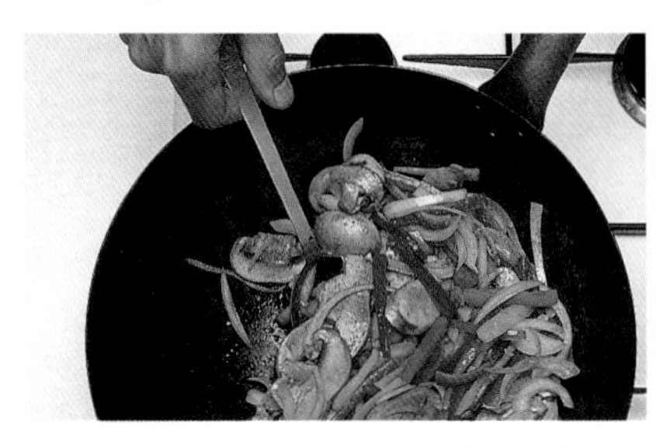

4 Heat a frying pan or wok until very hot. Add the marinated vegetables and stir-fry over high heat for 5–6 minutes, until the mushrooms and peppers are just tender. Season well. Spoon a little of the filling on to each tortilla and roll up. Garnish with fresh coriander and lime wedges and serve with the guacamole.

Chilli Beans with Basmati Rice

Red kidney beans, tomatoes and chilli make a great combination. Serve with pasta or pitta bread instead of rice, if you prefer.

Serves 4

INGREDIENTS
350 g/12 oz/2 cups basmati rice
30 ml/2 tbsp olive oil
1 large onion, chopped
1 garlic clove, crushed
15 ml/1 tbsp hot chilli powder
15 ml/1 tbsp plain flour
15 ml/1 tbsp tomato purée
400 g/14 oz can chopped tomatoes
400 g/14 oz can red kidney beans, rinsed and drained
150 ml/¼ pint/⅔ cup hot vegetable stock
salt and freshly ground black pepper
chopped fresh parsley, to garnish

1 Wash the rice several times under cold running water. Drain and cook in a pan of simmering water for 10–12 minutes, until tender. Drain and keep warm. Meanwhile, heat the oil in a frying pan. Add the onion and garlic and cook for 2 minutes.

2 Stir the chilli powder and flour into the onion and garlic mixture. Cook gently for 2 minutes, stirring frequently.

3 Stir in the tomato purée and chopped tomatoes. Add the kidney beans and hot vegetable stock. Cover and cook gently for 12 minutes, stirring occasionally.

4 Season the chilli sauce with salt and freshly ground black pepper. Drain the rice and serve at once, with the chilli beans, sprinkled with a little chopped fresh parsley.

Greek Spinach & Cheese Pies

These classic, savoury pies make a delicious, special-occasion main course. Any extras can be frozen before cooking.

Makes 4

INGREDIENTS
15 ml/1 tbsp olive oil
1 small onion, finely chopped
275 g/10 oz spinach, stalks removed
50 g/2 oz/4 tbsp butter, melted
4 sheets filo pastry,
about 45 x 25 cm/18 x 10 in
1 egg
large pinch of grated nutmeg
75 g/3 oz/¾ cup crumbled feta cheese
15 ml/1 tbsp grated Parmesan cheese
salt and freshly ground black pepper

1 Preheat the oven to 190°C/375°F/Gas 5. Heat the oil in a pan, add the onion and fry gently for 5–6 minutes, until softened. Add the spinach leaves and cook, stirring, until the spinach has wilted and some of the liquid evaporated. Leave to cool.

2 Brush four 10 cm/4 in diameter loose-based tartlet tins with a little melted butter. Take two sheets of the filo pastry and cut each into eight 11 cm/4¼ in squares. Keep the remaining sheets covered.

3 Brush four squares at a time with melted butter. Line the first tartlet tin with one square, gently easing it into the base and up the sides. Leave the edges overhanging.

4 Place the remaining three buttered squares on top of the first, turning them so the corners form a star shape. Repeat for the remaining tartlet tins.

5 Beat the egg with the nutmeg and seasoning, then stir in the cheeses and spinach. Divide the mixture among the tins and level smooth. Fold the overhanging pastry back over the filling.

6 Cut one of the remaining sheets of pastry into eight 10 cm/4 in rounds. Brush with butter and place two on top of each tartlet. Press around the edges to seal. Brush the remaining sheet of pastry with butter and cut into strips. Gently twist each strip and lay on top of the tartlets. Leave to stand for 5 minutes, then bake for about 30–35 minutes, until golden. Serve hot or cold.

Parsnip & Pecan Gougères with Watercress & Rocket Sauce

These scrumptious, nutty puffs conceal a surprisingly sweet parsnip centre.

Makes 18

INGREDIENTS
115 g/4 oz/½ cup butter
300 ml/½ pint/1¼ cups water
75 g/3 oz/¾ cup plain flour
50 g/2 oz/½ cup wholemeal flour
3 eggs, beaten
25 g/1 oz/¼ cup Cheddar cheese, grated
pinch of cayenne pepper or paprika
75 g/3 oz/¾ cup pecan nuts, chopped
1 medium parsnip, cut into
18 x 2 cm/¾ in pieces
15 ml/1 tbsp skimmed milk
10 ml/2 tsp sesame seeds
watercress sprigs, to garnish

FOR THE SAUCE
150 g/5 oz watercress, trimmed
150 g/5 oz rocket, trimmed
175 ml/6 fl oz/¾ cup plain yogurt
salt, freshly grated nutmeg
and freshly ground black pepper

1 Preheat the oven to 200°C/400°F/Gas 6. Place the butter and water in a pan. Bring to the boil and add all the flour in one go. Beat vigorously until the mixture leaves the sides of the pan and forms a ball. Remove from the heat and allow the mixture to cool slightly. Beat in the eggs a little at a time until the mixture is shiny and soft enough to fall gently from a spoon.

2 Beat in the Cheddar, cayenne or paprika and the nuts.

3 Lightly grease a baking sheet and drop on to it 18 heaped tablespoons of the mixture. Place a piece of parsnip on each and top with another heaped tablespoon of the mixture.

4 Brush the gougères with a little milk and sprinkle each one with sesame seeds. Bake in the preheated oven for 25–30 minutes, until puffed up, firm and golden.

5 Boil a pan of water and blanch the watercress and rocket for 2–3 minutes. Drain and immediately refresh in cold water. Drain well and chop.

6 Purée the trimmed watercress and rocket in a blender or food processor with the plain yogurt until smooth. Season to taste with salt, freshly grated nutmeg and pepper.

7 To reheat the sauce, place it in a bowl over a gently simmering pan of water and heat, taking care not to let it curdle. Serve with the gougères, garnished with watercress sprigs.

Roast Asparagus Crêpes

Roast asparagus is delicious and good enough to eat just as it comes. However, for a really splendid dinner-party dish, try this simple recipe.

Serves 6

INGREDIENTS
90–120 ml/6–8 tbsp olive oil
450 g/1 lb asparagus
175 g/6 oz/¾ cup mascarpone cheese
60 ml/4 tbsp single cream
25 g/1 oz/⅓ cup Parmesan cheese, grated
salt and freshly ground black pepper

FOR THE PANCAKES
175 g/6 oz/1½ cups plain flour
salt
2 eggs
350 ml/12 fl oz/1½ cups milk
vegetable oil, for frying

1 To make the pancake batter, mix the flour with a pinch of salt in a large bowl, food processor or blender, then add the eggs and milk and blend to make a smooth, fairly thin batter.

2 Heat a little oil in a large frying pan and add a small amount of batter, swirling the pan to coat the base evenly. Cook over a moderate heat for about 1 minute, then flip over with a spatula and cook the other side until golden. Set aside and cook the rest of the pancakes in the same way; the mixture makes about six large or 12 smaller pancakes.

3 Preheat the oven to 180°C/350°F/Gas 4 and lightly grease a large, shallow ovenproof dish or roasting tin with some of the olive oil.

4 Trim the asparagus by placing on a board and cutting off the bases. Using a small, sharp knife, peel away the woody ends, if necessary.

5 Arrange the asparagus in a single layer in the dish, trickle over the remaining olive oil, rolling the asparagus to coat each one thoroughly. Sprinkle with a little salt and roast in the oven for about 8–12 minutes, until tender (the cooking time depends on the stem thickness).

6 Blend the mascarpone cheese with the cream and Parmesan cheese and spread a generous tablespoonful over each of the pancakes, reserving a little for the topping. Preheat the grill.

7 Divide the asparagus spears among the pancakes, roll up and arrange in a single layer in an ovenproof dish. Spoon the reserved cheese mixture over the pancakes and place under a moderate grill for 4–5 minutes, until heated through and golden brown. Season with pepper and serve at once.

Leek Soufflé

A soufflé like this makes an impressive dinner-party dish and is really not difficult, but it must be served as soon as it is cooked.

Serves 2–3

INGREDIENTS
15 ml/1 tbsp sunflower oil
40 g/1½ oz/3 tbsp butter, plus extra for greasing
2 leeks, thinly sliced
about 300 ml/½ pint/1¼ cups milk
25 g/1 oz/¼ cup plain flour
4 eggs, separated
75 g/3 oz/¾ cup Gruyère cheese, grated
salt and freshly ground black pepper

1 Preheat the oven to 180°C/350°F/Gas 4 and butter a large soufflé dish. Heat the oil and 15 g/½ oz/1 tbsp of the butter in a small saucepan or flameproof casserole and fry the leeks over a gentle heat for 4–5 minutes, until soft but not brown, stirring occasionally.

2 Stir in the milk and bring to the boil. Cover and simmer for 4–5 minutes, until the leeks are tender. Strain the milk through a sieve into a measuring jug.

3 Melt the remaining butter in a saucepan, stir in the flour and cook for 1 minute. Remove pan from the heat. Make up the reserved milk with more milk to 300 ml/½ pint/1¼ cups. Gradually stir this into the pan to make a smooth sauce. Return to the heat and bring to the boil, stirring. When thickened, remove from the heat. Cool slightly and then beat in the egg yolks, cheese and leeks.

4 Whisk the egg whites until stiff and, using a large metal spoon, fold into the leek and egg mixture. Pour into the prepared soufflé dish and bake in the oven for about 30 minutes, until golden and puffy. Serve immediately.

Mushroom Tart

A rich, elegant tart made with wild mushrooms.

Serves 4

INGREDIENTS
350 g/12 oz shortcrust pastry, thawed if frozen
50 g/2 oz/4 tbsp unsalted butter
3 medium onions, halved and sliced
350 g/12 oz/4 cups assorted wild mushrooms such as ceps, morels, chanterelles, saffron milk-caps, oyster and field, sliced
leaves of 1 fresh thyme sprig, chopped
pinch of grated nutmeg
50 ml/2 fl oz/½ cup full-fat milk
50 ml/2 fl oz/½ cup single cream
1 egg and 2 egg yolks
salt and freshly ground black pepper

1 Preheat the oven to 190°C/375°F/Gas 5 and lightly grease a 23 cm/9 in loose-bottomed flan tin with butter. Roll out the pastry on a lightly floured surface and line the tin. Rest the pastry in the fridge for 1 hour.

2 Line the pastry case with greaseproof paper, fill with baking beans and/or pasta and bake blind for 25 minutes. Lift out the paper with the beans and pasta and leave to cool.

3 Melt the butter in a frying pan, add the onions, cover and cook slowly for 20 minutes. Add the mushrooms and thyme and continue cooking for a further 10 minutes. Season with salt, pepper and nutmeg.

4 Place the milk and cream in a jug and beat in the egg and egg yolks with a whisk. Place the mushroom mixture in the flan case and then pour over the milk and egg mixture. Bake for 15–20 minutes, until the centre is firm to the touch.

COOK'S TIP: To prepare ahead, the flan case can be part-baked and the filling made in advance. Continue from step 4.

Saffron Risotto

Italian risottos have a distinctive, creamy texture that is achieved by using arborio rice, a short grain rice which absorbs plenty of stock.

Serves 4

INGREDIENTS
5 ml/1 tsp (or 1 sachet) saffron strands
25 g/1 oz/2 tbsp butter
1 large onion, finely chopped
275 g/10 oz/1½ cups arborio rice
150 ml/¼ pint/⅔ cup dry white wine
1 litre/1¾ pints/4 cups vegetable stock
salt and freshly ground black pepper
Parmesan cheese shavings

FOR THE GREMOLATA
2 garlic cloves, crushed
60 ml/4 tbsp chopped fresh parsley
finely grated rind of 1 lemon

1 To make the gremolata, mix together the garlic, parsley and lemon rind. Set aside.

2 To make the risotto, put the saffron in a small bowl with 15 ml/1 tbsp boiling water and leave to stand. Melt the butter in a heavy-based saucepan and gently fry the onion for 5 minutes.

3 Stir in the rice and cook for about 2 minutes, until it becomes translucent. Add the wine and saffron mixture and cook for several minutes, until the wine is absorbed.

4 Add 600 ml/1 pint/2½ cups of the vegetable stock to the pan and simmer gently until the stock is absorbed, stirring frequently.

5 Gradually add more stock, a ladleful at a time, until the rice is tender. (The rice might be tender and creamy before you've added all the stock, so add it slowly towards the end of the cooking time.)

6 Season the risotto with salt and pepper and transfer to a serving dish. Scatter lavishly with shavings of Parmesan cheese and the gremolata.

VARIATION: If preferred, stir plenty of grated Parmesan cheese into the risotto.

Party Moussaka

Always a popular favourite with both guests and the cook at parties, moussaka is ideal because it benefits from being made ahead of time, requiring just reheating on the day.

Serves 8

INGREDIENTS

2 large aubergines, thinly sliced
6 courgettes, cut in chunks
about 150 ml/¼ pint/⅔ cup olive oil
675 g/1½ lb potatoes, thinly sliced
2 onions, sliced
3 garlic cloves, crushed
150 ml/¼ pint/⅔ cup dry white wine
2 x 400 g/14 oz cans chopped tomatoes
30 ml/2 tbsp tomato purée
425 g/15 oz can green lentils
10 ml/2 tsp dried oregano
60 ml/4 tbsp chopped fresh parsley
225 g/8 oz/2 cups feta cheese, crumbled
salt and freshly ground black pepper

FOR THE BECHAMEL SAUCE

40 g/1½ oz/3 tbsp butter
40 g/1½ oz/4 tbsp plain flour
600 ml/1 pint/2½ cups milk
freshly grated nutmeg
2 eggs, beaten
115 g/4 oz/1¼ cups Parmesan cheese, grated

1 Lightly salt the aubergines and courgettes in a colander and leave them to drain for 30 minutes. Rinse and pat dry with kitchen paper.

2 Heat the oil until quite hot in a frying pan and quickly brown the aubergine and courgette slices. Remove them with a slotted spoon and drain on kitchen paper. This step is important to cut down on the oiliness of the aubergine.

3 Next, brown the potato slices and drain on kitchen paper. Fry the onion and garlic with a little extra oil, for about 5 minutes, or until lightly browned. Pour in the wine and reduce, then add the tomatoes and their liquor, tomato purée and lentils. Stir in the herbs and season well. Cover and simmer for 15 minutes.

4 In a large, ovenproof dish, layer the vegetables, trickling the tomato and lentil sauce in between and scattering over the feta cheese. Finish with a layer of aubergine slices.

5 Cover the vegetables with a sheet of foil and bake at 190°C/375°F/ Gas 5 for 25 minutes, or until the vegetables are just cooked.

6 Meanwhile, for the béchamel sauce, put the butter, flour and milk into a saucepan and bring slowly to a boil, stirring or whisking constantly. The mixture should thicken and become smooth. Season and add nutmeg.

7 Remove the sauce from the heat and cool for 5 minutes, then beat in the eggs. Pour evenly over the vegetables and sprinkle with the grated Parmesan. If cooking ahead, cool and chill at this stage until required. To finish, return to the oven uncovered and bake for a further 25–30 minutes, until golden brown and bubbling hot. Remove from the oven and allow to stand for a few minutes before serving.

Pumpkin Filled with Vegetables & Pasta Shells

Glorious pumpkin shells summon up the delights of autumn and seem too good simply to throw away. Use one instead as a serving pot. Pumpkin and pasta make marvellous partners, especially as a main course served from the baked shell.

Serves 4

INGREDIENTS
2 kg/4½ lb pumpkin
1 onion, sliced
2.5 cm/1 in cube fresh root ginger
45ml/3 tbsp extra virgin olive oil
1 courgette, sliced
115 g/4 oz/¾ cup sliced mushrooms
400 g/14 oz can chopped tomatoes
75 g/3 oz/1 cup pasta shells
450 ml/¾ pint/2 cups vegetable stock
60 ml/4 tbsp fromage frais
30 ml/2 tbsp chopped fresh basil
salt and freshly ground black pepper

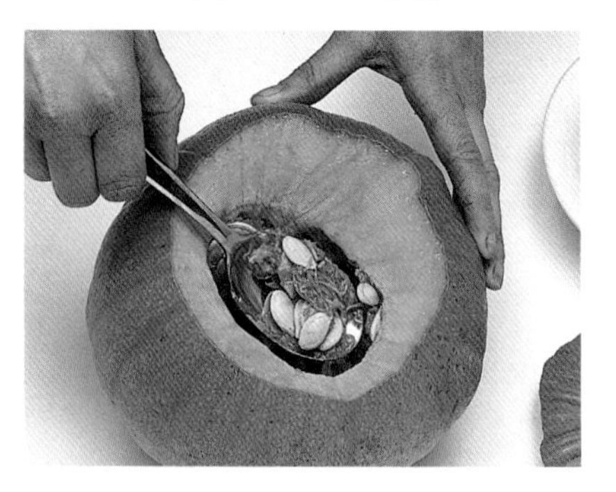

1 Preheat the oven to 180°C/350°F/ Gas 4. Cut the top off the pumpkin with a large, sharp knife and scoop out and discard the seeds.

2 Using a small, sharp knife and a sturdy tablespoon extract as much of the pumpkin flesh as possible, then chop it into even-size chunks.

3 Bake the pumpkin shell with its lid on for 45 minutes–1 hour, until the inside begins to soften when pierced with a knife.

4 Meanwhile, make the filling. Gently fry the onion, ginger and pumpkin flesh in the olive oil for about 10 minutes, stirring occasionally until the onion is soft.

5 Add the courgette and mushrooms and cook for a further 3 minutes, then stir in the tomatoes, pasta shells and vegetable stock. Season well with salt and pepper. Bring to the boil, cover and simmer over a gentle heat for 10 minutes.

6 Stir the fromage frais and chopped fresh basil into the pasta and spoon the mixture into the pumpkin. (It may not be possible to fit all the filling into the pumpkin shell, so serve the rest separately if this is the case.)

Ratatouille

This classic combination of colourful Mediterranean summer vegetables is infinitely flexible. Use the basic recipe as a guide for making the most of the vegetables you have on hand.

Serves 6

INGREDIENTS
2 medium aubergines, about 450 g/1 lb total
60–75 ml/4–5 tbsp olive oil
1 large onion, halved and sliced
2 or 3 garlic cloves, very finely chopped
1 large red or yellow pepper, seeded and cut into thin strips
2 large courgettes, cut into 1 cm/½ in slices
675 g/1½ lb ripe tomatoes, peeled, seeded and chopped, or 400 g/14 oz can chopped tomatoes
5 ml/1 tsp dried mixed herbs
salt and freshly ground black pepper

1 Preheat the grill. Cut the aubergine into 2 cm/¾ in slices, then brush the slices with olive oil on both sides and grill until lightly browned, turning once. Cut the slices into cubes.

2 Heat 15 ml/1 tbsp of the olive oil in a large, heavy saucepan or flameproof casserole and cook the onion over a medium-low heat for about 10 minutes, until softened and lightly golden, stirring frequently. Add the garlic, red or yellow pepper and courgettes and cook for a further 10 minutes, stirring occasionally.

3 Add the tomatoes and aubergine cubes, dried herbs and salt and pepper and simmer gently, covered, over a low heat for about 20 minutes, stirring occasionally. Uncover and continue cooking for a further 20–25 minutes, stirring occasionally, until all the vegetables are tender and the cooking liquid has thickened slightly. Serve hot or at room temperature.

COOK'S TIP: To remove the pepper skin and add flavour to the ratatouille, quarter the pepper and grill, skin-side up, until blackened. Enclose in a sturdy polythene bag and set aside until cool. Peel off the skin, then remove the core and seeds and cut the flesh into strips. Add to the vegetable mixture with the cooked aubergine.

Spinach Dhal

There are many different types of dhals eaten in India and each region has its own speciality. This is a delicious, lightly spiced dish with a mild, nutty flavour from the lentils, which combine well with the spinach.

Serves 4

INGREDIENTS
175 g/6 oz/1 cup chana dhal or yellow split peas
30 ml/2 tbsp oil
1.5 ml/¼ tsp black mustard seeds
1 onion, thinly sliced
2 garlic cloves, crushed
2.5 cm/1 in piece fresh root ginger, grated
1 red chilli, finely chopped
275 g/10 oz frozen spinach, thawed
1.5 ml/¼ tsp chilli powder
2.5 ml/½ tsp ground coriander
2.5 ml/½ tsp garam masala
2.5 ml/½ tsp salt

1 Wash the dhal or split peas in cold water. Put into a bowl and cover with water. Leave for 30 minutes.

2 Drain the dhal or peas and put in a saucepan with 175 ml/6 fl oz/¾ cup fresh water. Bring to the boil, cover, and simmer for 25 minutes.

3 Meanwhile, heat the oil in a large frying pan and fry the mustard seeds for 2 minutes, until they begin to splutter. Add the onion, garlic, ginger and chilli and fry for 5–6 minutes. Add the spinach and cook for 10 minutes, or until the spinach is dry and the liquid has been absorbed. Stir in the remaining spices and salt and cook for 2–3 minutes.

4 Drain the chana dhal or split peas, add to the spinach and cook for about 5 minutes. Serve at once.

Indian Spiced Okra with Almonds

It's not surprising that these long, elegantly shaped vegetables have the popular name of lady's fingers. Although commonly used in many international dishes, okra are particularly good with Indian spices.

Serves 2–4

INGREDIENTS
225 g/8 oz okra
50 g/2 oz/½ cup blanched almonds, chopped
25 g/1 oz/2 tbsp butter
15 ml/1 tbsp sunflower oil
2 garlic cloves, crushed
2.5 cm/1 in cube fresh root ginger, grated
5 ml/1 tsp cumin seeds
5 ml/1 tsp ground coriander
5 ml/1 tsp paprika
salt and freshly ground black pepper

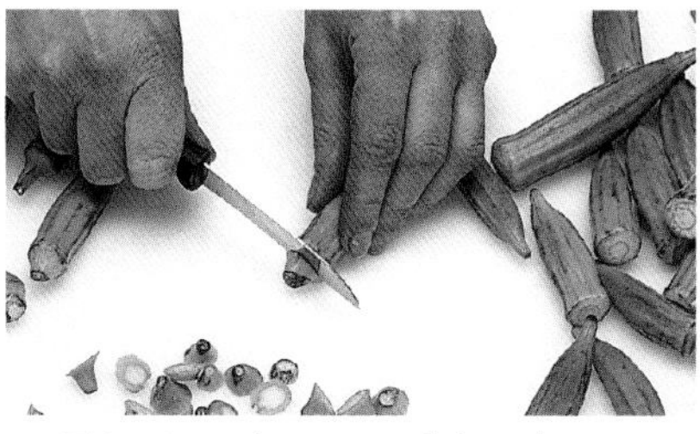

1 Trim just the tops of the okra stems and around the edges of the stalks. They have a sticky liquid which oozes out if prepared too far ahead, so trim them immediately before cooking.

2 In a shallow, flameproof casserole, fry the almonds in the butter until they are lightly golden, then remove and set aside.

3 Add the sunflower oil to the casserole and fry the okra, stirring constantly, for 2 minutes.

4 Add the garlic and ginger and fry gently for a minute, then add the spices and cook for another minute or so, stirring all the time.

5 Pour in about 300 ml/½ pint/1¼ cups water. Season well, cover and simmer for about 5 minutes or so, until the okra feel just tender.

6 Finally, mix in the fried almonds and serve piping hot.

Roasted Potatoes with Red Onions

Use small, waxy potatoes for this delicious vegetable dish.

Serves 4

INGREDIENTS
675 g/1½ lb small waxy potatoes
25 g/1 oz/2 tbsp butter
30 ml/2 tbsp olive oil
2 red onions, cut into chunks
8 garlic cloves, unpeeled
30 ml/2 tbsp chopped
fresh rosemary
salt and freshly ground black pepper

1 Preheat the oven to 230°C/450°F/ Gas 8. Peel and quarter the potatoes, rinse them well and pat thoroughly dry with a tea towel or on kitchen paper. Put the butter and oil in a roasting tin and place in the oven for 2 minutes to heat.

2 When the butter has melted, add the potatoes, red onions, garlic and rosemary. Toss well, then spread out in one layer.

3 Place in the oven for about 25 minutes, until the potatoes are golden and tender. Shake the tin from time to time to redistribute the potatoes. When cooked, season with salt and pepper and serve.

COOK'S TIP: For really crisp potatoes, make sure that they are completely dry before cooking. Resist the urge to turn the potatoes too often. Do not salt the potatoes until the end of cooking.

Green Beans with Tomatoes

This summer favourite uses ripe plum tomatoes and French beans.

Serves 4

INGREDIENTS
30 ml/2 tbsp olive oil
1 large onion, finely sliced
2 garlic cloves, finely chopped
6 large ripe plum tomatoes, peeled, seeded and coarsely chopped
150 ml/¼ pint/⅔ cup dry white wine
450 g/1 lb French green beans, sliced in half lengthways
16 stoned black olives
10 ml/2 tsp lemon juice
salt and freshly ground black pepper

1 Heat the oil in a large frying pan. Add the onion and garlic and cook for about 5 minutes, until the onion is softened but not brown.

2 Add the chopped fresh plum tomatoes, white wine, sliced French green beans, black olives and lemon juice and cook over a gentle heat for a further 20 minutes. Stir the vegetables from time to time, until the sauce is thickened and the beans are just tender. Season with salt and black pepper to taste and serve as a side dish.

COOK'S TIP: French beans need little preparation and now that they are grown without the string you simply have to top and tail them. When choosing, make sure that the beans snap easily – this is a good sign of freshness.

Garden Salad & Crostini

A colourful mixture of salad leaves topped with crispy bread crostini.

Serves 4–6

INGREDIENTS

3 thick slices day-old bread, such as ciabatta
120 ml/4 fl oz/½ cup extra virgin olive oil
garlic clove, cut in half
½ small Cos lettuce
½ small oak leaf lettuce
25 g/1 oz rocket leaves or cress
25 g/1 oz fresh flat leaf parsley
a few nasturtium leaves
edible flowers such as pansy and pot marigold
a small handful of young dandelion leaves
juice of 1 fresh lemon
sea salt flakes and freshly ground black pepper

1 Cut the bread into medium-size dice about 1 cm/½ in square.

2 Heat half the oil in a frying pan and fry the bread cubes in it, tossing them until they are well coated and lightly browned. Remove and cool.

3 Rub the inside of a large salad bowl with the garlic and discard. Pour the rest of the oil into the bottom of the bowl.

4 Wash, dry and tear the salad leaves into bite-size pieces and pile them into the bowl. Season with salt and pepper. Cover and chill until ready to serve. To serve, toss the salad in the oil at the bottom of the bowl, then sprinkle with the lemon juice and

Fresh Spinach & Avocado Salad

Young, tender spinach leaves make a change from lettuce in this salad.

Serves 2–3

INGREDIENTS
1 large avocado
juice of 1 lime
225 g/8 oz baby spinach leaves
115 g/4 oz cherry tomatoes
4 spring onions, sliced
½ cucumber, cut into chunks
50 g/2 oz radishes, sliced

FOR THE DRESSING
115 g/4 oz soft silken tofu
45ml/3 tbsp milk, plus a little extra
10 ml/2 tsp mustard
2.5 ml/½ tsp white wine vinegar
pinch of cayenne pepper
salt and freshly ground black pepper

1 Halve, stone and skin the avocado. Cut the flesh into slices. Transfer to a plate, and drizzle over the lime juice. Wash and dry the spinach leaves. Put them in a large bowl.

2 Cut the larger cherry tomatoes in half and add all the tomatoes to the bowl with the spring onions, cucumber and sliced radishes.

3 To make the dressing, put all the ingredients in a food processor or blender. Process until smooth and creamy. Scrape the dressing into a bowl and add some more milk if you like a thinner dressing. Sprinkle with a little extra cayenne pepper. Serve with the salad.

Index

This edition published by Hermes House

Hermes House is an imprint of
Anness Publishing Limited
Hermes House, 88–89 Blackfriars Road, London SE1 8HA

Publisher: Joanna Lorenz
Editor: Valerie Ferguson
Series Designer: Bobbie Colgate Stone
Designer: Andrew Heath
Production Controller: Joanna King

Recipes contributed by: Catherine Atkinson, Angela Boggiano, Carla Capalbo, Carole Clements, Roz Denny, Nicola Diggins, Matthew Drennan, Joanna Farrow, Sarah Gates, Shirley Gill, Christine Ingram, Marisha Kanani, Soheila Kimberley, Annie Nichols, Maggie Pannell, Anne Sheasby, Steven Wheeler, Elizabeth Wolf-Cohen, Jeni Wright.

Photography: Karl Adamson, Edward Allwright, Steve Baxter, James Duncan, Michelle Garrett, Amanda Heywood, Janine Hosegood, David Jordan, Patrick McLeavey, Michael Michaels

2 3 4 5 6 7 8 9 10

Notes:

For all recipes, quantities are given in both metric and imperial measures and, where appropriate, measures are also given in standard cups and spoons. Follow one set, but not a mixture, because they are not interchangeable.

Standard spoon and cup measures are level.

1 tsp = 5 ml 1 tbsp = 15 ml

1 cup = 250 ml/8 fl oz

Australian standard tablespoons are 20 ml. Australian readers should use 3 tsp in place of 1 tbsp for measuring small quantities of gelatine, cornflour, salt, etc.

Medium eggs are used unless otherwise stated.

Printed and bound in China